the light user scheme

the light user scheme
Richard Skinner

Published 2013 by
Smokestack Books
PO Box 408, Middlesbrough TS5 6WA
e-mail: info@smokestack-books.co.uk
www.smokestack-books.co.uk

the light user scheme
Cover image: John Cage, *10 Stones 2*
Author photo: Keith Didcock

Printed and bound in the U.K.
by Martins the Printers Ltd,
Berwick upon Tweed.

ISBN 978-0-9571722-9-6

Middlesbrough
moving forward

Smokestack Books is represented
by Inpress Ltd
www.inpressbooks.co.uk

Acknowledgements

Some of these poems have previously appeared in *First Pressings, Staple 69/70* and on the CD release, *all she wants grows blue*, by Pablo's Eye. Thanks to those editors – Lee Brackstone and Wayne Burrows – and also to Axel Libeert. Thanks to Andy Croft at Smokestack. Grateful acknowledgement is made to the John Cage Trust for their kind permission to reproduce *10 Stones 2*, with thanks to Laura Kuhn. My thanks also go to Jacqueline Crooks, Christian Patracchini and Becky Swift for their love and support.

*'Poets are more concerned with arranging images
than with creating them.'*

Viktor Shklovsky

Contents

all she wants grows blue

She would stand alone in front of a mirror, stroking her belly,
    looking for signs.
She was puzzled by the expression she saw there.

Later, he climbed up to the bridge and looked out over the city.
It was night and the city orange.
The river swelled, folding in on itself, like muscles.

izba

She wouldn't be leaving Russia now, she said, though she often
    thought she would.

I try to imagine the house in 1944 – her lithe and tanned,
listening to the radio, teaching her son mathematics, while her
    husband
spent the days trying to reach his dead brothers.

The summer grass yellowing in the meadows behind.

She was catching crayfish with her son when he finally
    understood
that the afterlife is what we leave in others.

esther

She woke up and was certain of it, she understood the situation.
She walked all day, distracted. She felt the connection.

She saw the long figure in white. She remembered so she
    wouldn't forget.

She pictures the shoes of the nurse, the way the mud adheres.
She touched the uniform, dirty and wet.

She began to feel guilty, she felt it was her fault.
The way that lives intersect.

the deep, dark days of september

We used to play in the orchards, when the apples were green.
The light was sharp, our eyes were open.

Years later, birds flew south. I remember sleeping badly that
night.

The house was empty when the apples eventually fell,
red and blind.

a way you'll never be

She sits at the table, watching the street.
She looks at the faces passing by – each one a clock.

Higher up, the sun hits a cornice. A jet shines silver.

She wears only blue socks now,
and has been filling the gaps ever since.

the dark insects of happiness

What peace is there in a deep place?

For the first time in years, the earth shook today and, as it did,
I saw my feet grow smaller
and my uncles come back to life.

My wife calms me. She says
'Don't run after things – let them seep in.
Build yourself on white, this quiet and this stillness.'

the secret springs of action

Three days later, he still hoped there was something better in
    him,
something to save him.

He dreamt of rain falling on her bed.
He dreamt of women in coats picking apricots,
each one transparent and effervescent.

He had never dreamt of such enormity.
He never knew a worse man than himself.

vanishing point

The year before last, in some town or other,
you stopped me in the quiet square:
by a stone fountain, a woman was drinking.

I stooped to watch her hands gripping the edge,
I saw a lizard dart across her back.

Somewhere, way off, a girl cried.

the blue hour

At the basin, he scrubs his hands, trying to
rid himself of his grandfather's stain.
He scrapes, but the errors remain.

Next day, he rose at dawn, refreshed.
He went outside and looked around –
he realised his life would not be his to keep.

a remoteness from the centre

And so they sat, watching the waves break.
He picked up green pebbles and threw them into the sea,
she played with her jade earrings.

That night in bed, she felt one missing.

She pictured it lying in the sea,
she felt relief:
the best place to hide a leaf is in a tree.

the first principle of justice

In the sense that understanding is movement,
whoever understands themselves, moves themselves.

I took your head in my hands
and felt the thunder of yesterday there –
you're thinner now, but the distance travelled is in your eyes.

We can only understand what we already know.

a waltz

They arrive in the white city after months of travel,
they've heard it is a place far from decisions.

His daughter is seeing snow for the first time –
she hasn't said a word all day.

He thinks about consequences. Randomness.

He sees the city as a knot of roads,
his life written on her white mind.

an object seen for the first time

The white nuns walk in prayer, circling a pool
while silver fish swim in the water.

I sit in their cool, spherical garden, against a tall, straight tree. I
    decide
I am everything at once,
not separate parts placed separately.

A nun shows me to a round, white table and I see
six silver fish, dying.

forêt en montagne, l'hiver, avant 1928

I sit in the sun and hear, high up and somewhere behind me,
a woman singing an old melody.

I read the paper, about a woman found dead in the woods.
Where have I heard that song?

In the afternoon, I walk high above the snowline, through pines.
I come to a clearing with a splash of red, like vanilla ice cream
with a dash of raspberry.

heads

As she leans herself on him, he remembers
how her hair used to be long
during the years they lived in the city.

He has a photograph of her jumping from a wall.

Later that same day, they talked. He passed his hand through
    her hair
and meant to say he wanted to be free to be wrong.

an incident upriver

She reads his letter again, the first for many months –
he speaks of the strange flowers there, the wind at night.

As she reads, she has the sense of understanding;
she knows, before he has said, all that he sees.

His wishes are not inexplicable to her, just unexplained.

She inhales the scents of foreign towns,
lets the pages fall, crumbling like bones.

situation 40

While they work in the fields,
the huge, yellow butterflies come, wiping clear their minds.

He looks and tells her how Vinnie had gone mad with the colour.
He had said the yellow brings a happiness
difficult to explain because it's so easy to understand.

He still sees Vinnie, he says,
walking the line between sky and land.

a horn heard through fog

He used to feel as young as he was
when they pushed the boat out from the shore.
He remembers speaking and seeing her quietly watch his hands.

These days, he mostly stays at home, but sometimes
he pushes out the boat once more.

Then one day, he hears her kind words over his shoulder.
He looks from the sail to the land and knows he is older.

mu

She got up that morning and walked outside.
She went to the square and out of the town, she passed a cyclist
who said good morning.

By afternoon, she was under the mountains.
She crossed the bridge with a toothless cat on the wall.
She went into the woods and up to the grave.

She stood for a while, then stepped back and to the left.

twinning

After school, he took his crystals down to the sea and sat:
his eye understood their shape but his mind could not.

The blue was the colour of his teacher's wet eyes.

He held them to the sky where they disappeared –
their colours the same.
He put them in the sea where they dissolved –
one into the other.

the mute cause

As he cooks one morning, she walks into his house
and sits. He watches and talks to her
but she is silent and waiting.

Days pass. The wind blows through the open door.

He leaves his house, walks over hills
into a village below. One morning,
he enters a house, sits and waits.

brilliantine

He stopped her in that street and told her
'All this I have seen before'
and asked her to explain it.

She thought about the laws of time,
the day, in the park, when she cried without reason,

the book of inexplicable events he keeps from her,
open and unfairly close to his heart.

lupus street

The day after she left him, he lay on his bed.
He watched the ceiling and roused himself
only when the sun had set.

Two weeks later, he studied her brush all morning,
pulling out the hairs. Then he washed her sock.

Four months after, he left his room
and smashed every window in the block.

delay horizon

Driving one night in the rain, he nearly falls asleep.
He stops for coffee, looks at his hand.

He remembers that night together with her. When she thought
    him asleep,
she got up, stretched and touched the window –
he wondered what new weather she had divined.

Next morning, she woke him,
stroked his palm and told him the news.

the inevitable accumulation of detail

She dreamt of blue electricity, one dark night,
fizzing through her eyes and head.

The next evening, she walked
along the city river and comprehended the streetlights.
She looked at the dark sky and heard the trill
of young, white stars. She looked deeper and made out the hum
of stars older and red.

the divine cortex

At dusk, she walked along the wire fences
and saw a hole in the ground.
She thought of her grandfather, speechless
since his fall into a crater.

She imagines his silence at seeing the fire,
blooming like a flower,
at smelling the soft musk of explosions.

the decision tree

Her son is crying, so she strokes his cheek.
His eyes are the colour of the bird's eggs
she found one day with her uncle.

She wanted to touch them but he told her not to.
He reached up into the tree and then opened his hand –
she saw the smashed green eggs.
She looked at him and he began to laugh, quietly.

the fourth victim of circumstance

The woman collapsed in room 85
of the Leonora Hotel, in '53.

Just before, a man in a suit left the foyer.
The maid, when questioned, swore he had a ladder and spade.

Later, she talked to her friend about
the deep magnets that eyes are,
the dark attraction of corridors.

the adjuster

As a boy, Pedro had a stutter and loved straight lines.

When he married, he moved to the city for its
railings, striplights, roadsigns, ledges, doorways.

Pedro found he could talk smoothly after his son was born.

When Pablo was a child, he loved his father's singing,
but when it came to shoelaces,
he hid from his father and looked at them, confused.

the episodic nature of life

In Damascus, anatomy was discovered before Christ.

So Omar told me at school. I traced him
20 years later to Plymouth
where I'd heard he had an illegal practice.

I found him drunk in an off-limits bar
protesting that his name was Arabic for 'doctor',
but people were listening to a sermon on the radio.

ur-vignette

Her days became unbearably stretched.
Voices were sub-aquatic hums.
Sirens were two-note symphonies.
Breezes were polar storms.

Then, one morning, her skin righted itself.
She knew the gaps in her mind would slacken and fill –
she saw the sun rise, real and full.

the crush

She sits watching the snow fall
silently on the mountains.

She remembers her husband's quiet death in all that snow –
his axe a mile away.

She stands by the window and comes to see
she is separated from him now
by much much more than snow.

unresting

After she left, he stayed by the small river
and watched his small hands
creating confusion in the water.

He'd seen a programme the week before
about a Russian river, which froze every year.
Wolves lived there in winter, on the ice.
Nothing else.

a wind chill on wednesday

Two old women walk arm in arm,
Vera with a cane, Violet in pink shoes.

Years ago, Vera fell in love with a magician,
who spirited Violet away.

Later, she told Vera how to perform voodoo.
They drank vodka to the magician's memory –
told each other how much they missed him.

the hazchem building

He puts his fedora on and steps off the train.
As he exits the barrier, he clutches his case and checks for aliens.

In the sunny Viennese square,
the air around him cools. People shiver.

He kills time at the zoo. He eyes the ape.
Monkeys scream.

zah

In the morning, he picked up a hitcher,
who told him she loved maths and the sea.
He dropped her off at the interchange for the shore.

After stopping in the afternoon, he woke by the roadside
and realised he'd lost his wallet.

By night, he was lost in the hills. He couldn't remember
how much money he'd had, where the lake was.

tanzania, 1903

That summer, he watches his wife go yellow with jaundice.
He wheels her onto the veranda where, every evening,
she watches the yellowhammers gather in the trees.

One morning, her fever has gone.
He walks outside, not knowing who to thank. He looks around
    and sees
fifty-five yellowhammers, dead on the lawn.

aphasia

As the train moved, the old man opposite him looked out the
    window
and tapped his hearing aid all night.

Next morning, the old man is gone.
He looks out and sees the horizon always receding, he tries to
    imagine
what the old man saw.
He forgets that the world is only his mind
gone mad with remembering.

to cast

When she asked him why he was leaving,
he told her he hated her perfection.

Two years later, another woman asked him why.
He said he disliked her blue mood.

He began to travel.

On a plane one day, he became lonely when he read that,
five miles up, the perfect sky is always blue.

the green road

One day in December, Werther drew a line from his home to
hers.
He began to walk the line to keep her alive.

He met criminals, refugees and the meek. He met a dictator
who boasted that when he cried, children died.

On Christmas Day, he entered Winnersh. He walked to her
house and went in.
She lay, expecting him. He said his goodbyes. She stroked his
cheek
and then closed her eyes.

calf

He held his child and looked at her face.
Cool and distant, like the moon from the earth –
she was speechless from birth.

He smoothes her dress, sends her off to school.

He is calm that day, he thinks how
life's mysteries lie in blandness, that our hands
often travel where we wish them not.

the dressmaker

She spent her days spinning in the suburbs of Antwerp.
She loved her projects. She felt herself grow light and clear
as she smoothed out the slubs.

She forgot about the young man who used to call on her.

She loved being patient and empty. She didn't see, as she cut
    and sewed,
that her life was only a relief, not a cure.

a waterfall of hips

In the park, she walked down to her lake of sorrow
and saw energy in the ripples –
the disappointment their movement caused.

She greens the grass, sees the leaves blow across, like motors.

She felt anger rise within her, like an iguana,
saw the workings of days coursing before her,
like an autobahn someone had punched through her brain.

withiner

For five years he was locked away, while diplomats decided his
    future.
At first, he wept, thought of his father, his sister's cool heart.

Later, he calculated the sun's distance from the earth, mapped
    whole worlds
with sine curves on the wall. He held his life together, let it fall
    apart.

He talked to his invisible other, saw metals change colour.

When he was released, he stepped outside himself. At the
    airport, he knew
he could no longer arrive, only ever depart.

the mind cooler

He hears the shipping forecast for Scilly
Automatic
and imagines the rising thermals over Burundi,
the rainbow vent fields off the Azores.

He gets a call from his ex-wife;
she tells him she's feeling blue
sitting under the sumachs of Canada.

the marrow experience

Gene spent his childhood train-spotting with his father.
He learned about Charlie Bravo 303, the Sunliner 4
and yearned to be a driver.

One night, his father died of hammer blows to the head.

As a young man, Gene developed a stammer.
He avoided termini, was careful not to let
booming numbers and names destroy him.

the muscle flutter

She walked along the sides of motorways, watching the cars,
with too many feelings to know which one to follow
so that, for years, she merely endured.

Walking home, she saw red boxes on the sides of houses,
waiting to alarm. She turned a corner and saw a crash –
she inhaled when the man's legs collapsed like bellows.

Next morning, she woke up feeling fresher than before.

new feels

She spent years trying to be like her father. She admired his bulk,
the tautness of his mind, she didn't see the worry.

When she was twenty, she married a man like her father.
Years later, she realised he wasn't.

She divorced and moved in with her father. Only then
did she see how different they were.
Only then, did they like each other.

versions

He bought a new rose every week after his mother died
and wore it in his buttonhole every day to work.
After nine months he collapsed and sought help.

'Grief has its own time patterns,' the doctor said.

Nine months later, he went back to work.
He told everyone he was through buying roses
while touching the withered flower he kept in his pocket.

manor aquatics

She left her husband because she showed her true face to others
and came to lie to him.

In the Red Sea, she learnt to dive. At 50 metres, the red fish lost
    their colour.
At 80 metres, the blue. At 100 metres, there was nowhere to go.

She returned to her husband, and told him about the blackness
    there.
She cried. She told him about the strange white fish flashing in
    the ooze,
said she no longer had anything to hide.

rootwork

Monika had dyed blond hair and studied music. Her teacher
tried to win her. She let him love her, then moved on.

She studied, letting seven teachers win her and then crack.
After four years, she left the academy. The seven men chewed
on their minds and hurled questions at her back.

She spent the summer living with a boatman. They collected
   berries
on the islands, listened to the streams and winds. She let her
   hair go brown.

red-light returning

His father told him about his aviation days –
the 'red-outs' while doing wide loops.

They ran the boat out, chose an island from which to fish.
He went swimming, dropped two metres and felt the head-rush.

On the way back, he imagined the high-intensity lights on the
    tips of wings
that every good pilot turned on at landing.
Passing the buoys at dusk, he made sure to keep the red lights
    to their right.

the ready room

When they met, he told her his future was the same as her past
and moved in a week later. To prove his love, he painted one wall
'Sweet Briar' and the other 'Strawberry Fool'.

After months of lying alone in bed, she guessed
her entrance was his exit.
The moon shone on the walls, she looked but the light
showed no difference in the shades.

mule tours

As a boy, he saw a white horse plummet into water
and longed to join the circus in Colorado.

As an old man, he saw a white horse standing
just off Piccadilly Circus, with steam pluming from its back.

He thought the horse had maybe lived a double life
as he knew a crazy mother
would suspect of her wicked daughter.

coping styles

After seeing Tom die in battle, he found a scrap of paper
and wrote: fish, war, supper, friend, code.

Years later, he wrote a book about war. At a dinner
held in his honour, he made a speech, but no-one took heed.

He tipped the doorman, walked down to the beach.
He looked at the setting sun and said his creed.
He toasted Tom, then burnt his book.

the zest for ritual

He writes his grievances against her – to do with
sloth, vanity and debt. He feels a new sense of orderliness.
He shows it to her.

She reads it, says 'Are you trying to remember me
because you think I forget?'

After she's left, he finds a ring, a bill, a discarded dress.
He recalls her saying his list was really a litany.

the cedars of lebanon

He spent three days searching the Gospels for evidence of Judas but found none, except pointers to the blackness of his heart.

In the Old City, he counted the paper prayers between bricks before meeting an expert from the Seminary.

The expert listened, nodded and said 'Worry is a prayer for an act unwanted' and left. He saw him head west out of the city, beating his sheep with the blackest of sticks.

post-road downs

She saw the sleek black cars snake along the new motorway
and wondered at the precision of measuring speed.
She saw Orion wink through bits of cloud.

He was late for a meeting at the mortuary. He drove quickly
through the mist and thought about the formation of calendars.
He pictured Ptolemy watching Sirius rise
in the new month of January. Or was it February?

augury

He watches the ducks fly south now it's autumn –
necks like ladles, feet like forks.
He touches his dead wife's locket.

'It's only wild ducks that have red feet,' she had said.
He looked down at her yellow shoes last summer
and put a hand in her pocket.
'I'm tame,' she had said.

muzique mechanique

She sorts through her husband's things. A photo of Bruce Lee,
    circa '74
(she remembers 'karate' means 'empty hand'); a box of tricks;
a photo of Mount Fuji; a Malay singer in 1906.

He said he loved calligraphy for its distinction of what is
and isn't there – the difference between what used to be
and what is no more. Later, she holds his chop-sticks, like batons,
and remembers that 'karaoke' means 'empty orchestra'.

horological sundries

The Divisional Scene Examiner arrived at 2:40 am.
The woman, as old as his mother, was face down – the heavy clock
had tumbled and crushed her while she was winding it up.

She had the same name. Rosemary.

She used to listen to Big Ben on the radio, when he was a child in Sydney.
He studied Medicine, then left for London – he arrived at 7:33 am.
He walked up Whitehall and, when he heard the chimes of Big Ben, cried.

the suremixer

Because he believed in things, he took people at their word. Saints
and sinners were all the same to him. She, however, doubted things.

On a train one day, they saw a young man beat a child. He froze, she fumed.
He felt pain for the child, she challenged the young man.

In the witness box, he doubted his testimony and withdrew.
She was confident and sure –
she gloated at her words and the sentence she knew they would secure.

brain fag

'Perfection is death,' he said. She had been complaining
that he was too often wrong. He knew this was how they differed.

She loved getting things right. She called them good days, but
    really
they were all mediocre, he thought.

He loved bad days, full of error and conjecture.
She didn't realise that he did this on purpose. He'd always
    thought
the bad days were sugar daddies to the good.

a klaxon

The train leaves Blackheath, lurches under wet branches, round
    dead litter,
bare walls. People drift on and off at stations.

Just outside London Bridge, a jet crosses the sun, and,
for an instant, I'm sure I imagine it.

But last night, I am certain of it,
I woke and saw you staring at me, like a searchlight
that finds the wrecked plane, then moves on.

heterotactics

Anselm grew up in Dill, Indiana, until he became a star and
    moved out west.
For years, he employed his twin, Virginius, as a stand-in at
    dinners,
a body double in blue movies, a decoy for fans.

At the Oscars, Virginius blew his cover. He said he was merely a
    sex-doll
with Anselm as his lover. He thanked the audience and exited
    left.
The industry went wild. The Academy retired. Within the week
they announced Virginius as the year's Best Actor.

matters irie

Serge drove his cart every morning delivering milk. He talked
to his customers about astronomy and the weather.
One fine morning, his legs scissored and he collapsed –
a window in the street cracked and the sun went in.

His daughter, Cecile, stayed by his bed for three days.
On the fourth, a doctor showed her the X-rays. He pointed,
but she couldn't tell if the grey area was a tumour, a rainstorm
    or a galaxy.

a priestly demolition

Anne was stripping beds and listening to the radio when she
    heard raindrops
and a voice say: 'Simplify. Simplify.'
She stopped. Soon after, she ended certain friendships. She no
    longer shopped.

Two years later, alone at a Chinese restaurant called Blue Sky,
she unwrapped her fortune cookie, which read:
'You can have what you most want in the world, but not the
    second or third.'
Anne nodded to herself. 'I know. I know,' she said.

the cobalt motor hotel, toronto

'Those days are over,' said Mona,
leaning on the counter. The TV went fuzzy and died.

Mist descended on the corner of Bay and Bloor.
The monkey puzzle tree hunched down for the night.

'Who's like us?' Mona sighed.
'Only a few,' said Earl from his chair, 'and they're all dead.'

papa, antoine

He is always up before his wife, and reads in the kitchen
while its surfaces are clear and clean. Usually, he takes a walk
    beside the tidy lawns
as his children dress in mismatched clothes.

He has been afraid ever since the miscarriage and pills.
'We don't ever recover, we only ever replace,' he thinks
and carefully avoids slipping through the pavement grilles.

sultans

The blue-skinned Tuareg smiled and held out his hand,
'Welcome to Timbuktu, the mysterious city,' he said.

I had heard of eunuchs and unicorns, virgins and verdigris,
    instead
he led me through empty streets to the ruined mosque
where I brushed off showers of blood-red dust.

'C'est un grand nom,' the Tuareg laughed, 'mais c'est rien.'

clinique l'orangerie

Stan was born with a harelip. His mother lingered in the
    waiting room
as the doctors wheeled him into the theatre.
After the op, his father bought her a tulip.

At her funeral, Stan bought her four more.

Cleaning up the house after, he fingered the bottles of nail-
    polish remover,
then put them away with the mop and broom –
the smell had always reminded him of the ether.

the vague notion of authorship

Japanese scientists have recently confirmed my appearance,
    they say
that the papaya is not a cousin of passion fruit, but of the
    cauliflower,
that a cow is more akin to whales than camels.

As a foundling, I can now choose my inheritance – the Great
    Dane
and chihuahua share the same ancestor.
Roses are not like saxifrages, but buckthorns and nettles.

fisgård

Masatoshi went to Finland to bury his parents. He thought
it was the end of the world. After the burial, he met a sailor in a
 bar
who had been to Hokkaido. They got drunk together on 'Black
 Death'.
He told Masatoshi that, on Mercury, the days are longer than
 the years.

He said this Taoish thinking had been like a weapon for him.
It had dissolved the stones in his mind, it had solved dilemmas,
like the death of his parents one long night, years ago.

the garden of wear

One summer, Christian went swimming in the Baltic with his
    wife. A few days later,
he started falling over. He would suddenly trip and fold.
The doctor diagnosed labyrinthitis and ordered him to bed.

Every time he moved his head, the world would tip and slide.
The faces of his sisters exchanged places.
After six weeks, he stepped to a window and looked out. In the
    garden,
his mother and her nurse were sitting in the old light,
    comparing hands.